Adaptations

Monika Davies

Consultant

Jill Tobin
California Teacher of the Year
Semi-Finalist
Burbank Unified School District

Publishing Credits

Rachelle Cracchiolo, M.S.Ed., *Publisher*
Conni Medina, M.A.Ed., *Managing Editor*
Diana Kenney, M.A.Ed., NBCT, *Senior Editor*
Dona Herweck Rice, *Series Developer*
Robin Erickson, *Multimedia Designer*
Timothy Bradley, *Illustrator*

Image Credits: Cover, pp1. ap-images/iStock; p.21 David Aubrey / Science Source; p.7 Francesco Tomasinelli / Science Source; pp.2, 4, 5, 9, 10, 12, 13, 15, 17, 18, 20, 21, 22, 26, 27, 32 iStock; p.28, 29 J.J. Rudisill; p.23 Konrad Wothe / Minden Pictures /National Geographic Creative; p.11 Muriel Duhau / Science Source; p.6 Radarfoto / Alamy; p.25 Thomas Marent/ Minden Pictures/National Geographic Creative; all other images from Shutterstock.

Library of Congress Cataloging-in-Publication Data

Davies, Monika, author.
  Adaptations / Monika Davies.
    pages cm
  Summary: "Giraffes have long necks. Polar bears have thick fur and large feet. Octopuses change colors. All of these are adaptations. Adaptations help living things survive. Whether it's hiding from predators, the ability to catch prey, or traits that increase reproduction, adaptations are important"-- Provided by publisher.
  Audience: Ages 4-6.
  Includes index.
  ISBN 978-1-4807-4679-4 (pbk.) -- ISBN 1-4807-4679-7 (pbk.)
  1. Adaptation (Biology)--Juvenile literature. 2. Competition (Biology)--Juvenile literature. 3. Animals--Adaptation--Juvenile literature. I. Title.
  QH546.D38 2016
  578.4--dc23
                                    2014045202

Teacher Created Materials

5301 Oceanus Drive
Huntington Beach, CA 92649-1030
http://www.tcmpub.com
ISBN 978-1-4807-4679-4

Table of Contents

Making Changes

All living things change. Plants, animals—even you go through changes. Think about the ways you have changed over the past few years. Have you grown taller? Some changes may happen fast, and some are very slow. Either way, these **traits** and the way they change are what make you unique.

All living things have a set of traits. Traits are what make us different from one another. Traits include eye color. They also include curly, straight, or wavy hair. Animals have traits that include speed, eating preferences, and sleeping habits. Plants have traits that include petal color, leaf size, and temperature needs. Traits are passed from one generation to the next. These traits may change with each generation to help living things survive.

Happy Smells

Babies have developed a surprising and unique way to ensure attention—through scent. The smell of babies activates a part of the female brain that is related to cravings. Female brains react to babies the same way they do when they're craving food.

In 1835, Charles Darwin was the first person to study natural selection.

Adaptation

Sometimes, animals' environments change. It's important that they **adapt** to their new environments. A fire, a flood, or another natural disaster may change an animal's home. The animal must adapt to live in its new environment. If organisms don't adapt, they won't survive.

Species change slowly through natural selection. Through this process, plants and animals that are able to adapt survive, and those that cannot die. Think about a giraffe. A long time ago, the ancient giraffe had a short neck like other animals. But over the years, giraffes with longer necks were able to reach more food at the top of trees. They produced more **offspring** than the short-necked giraffes, and their babies also had long necks. This adaptation helped them survive.

Body and Mind

A physical adaptation is a change that affects an organism's body. A behavioral adaptation is a change in an organism's habits, or ways of doing something.

Finding a Niche

It is important for organisms to find a home that suits their individual traits and meets their needs. If they don't, they might die. Their bodies will have to find ways to survive in their **habitat**. Organisms must find their **niche** in their environment. It may be easy to get food in one place but difficult to find water. Organisms must adapt and find ways to get water. These adaptations help them survive. Remember the ancient giraffes? Those with the longest necks were able to reach the leaves at the top of trees. They passed the special trait of a long neck to their offspring. This trait helps the next generation fit into the niche.

Organisms have different traits that may change to ensure their survival. An adaptation may help an animal find food, or it may make it easier for them to hide from **predators**. It may keep the animal warm or help with reproduction. Adaptations enable living things to survive.

A Cool Trick

Most fish die when the water in their cells freezes. But, Arctic fish have adapted to icy waters. They have a kind of antifreeze in their cells to prevent their cells from freezing!

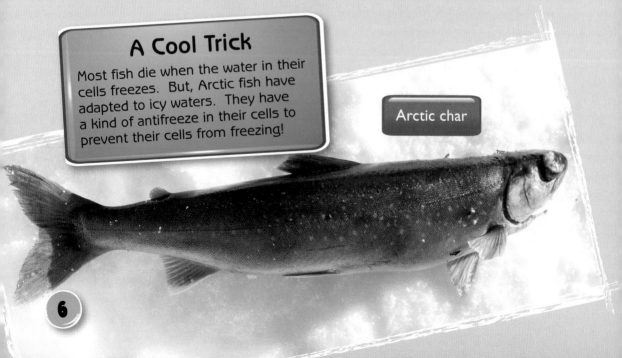

Arctic char

Malaysian orchid mantis

Ecology 101

Many people think an organism's habitat and niche are the same thing. But they aren't! Habitats are the places where plants and animals live. A niche is the part of the habitat that provides the things the plant or animal needs to live and survive. A habitat supports many species. A niche supports only one species.

Surviving in the Wild

Adaptations make it possible for organisms to survive on Earth. Each living creature has a unique set of features that make its life easier. But that doesn't mean survival is easy.

Fabulous Feet

As we grow, we learn new things. One of the first things humans learn to do is walk. Our feet are specially designed to help us balance and move. But every living creature has different feet. Habitats can vary widely. And feet have adapted across species to match each environment.

Polar bears are no exception. These majestic animals have feet adapted for a cold environment. The bottoms of their feet are covered with fur. This keeps them warm. They also have long claws that help them walk on ice and prevent them from slipping. Polar bears have large feet to match their massive bodies. This allows the weight of the animal to be spread out over more space, which prevents the ice from cracking. Their feet work just like snowshoes!

A squirrel has claws so it can scamper up a tree quickly and efficiently!

Walk Your Own Path

Animals adapt physically to their environment with the types of feet they have.

Cats and dogs have digitigrade posture. This means that the bones in their feet have adapted for them to stand with their weight on their toes. This helps them run to catch their prey. Some prey such as pigs and deer also have this adaptation to help them escape predators.

Ducks have webbed feet. The webbing helps them swim. Ducks use their webbed feet like paddles to push against the water.

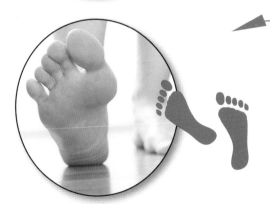

Humans, bears, and skunks are all plantigrade animals. Plantigrade animals walk with the toes and heel touching the ground. Animals with this adaptation usually don't require the speed of other animals. But they benefit from having a larger foot that holds their weight and provides stability.

Strong Swimmers

Not all animals live on land. There are some animals that live entirely underwater. These animals have adapted to their wet habitat.

Great white sharks are natural predators that live underwater. Like fish, sharks have a dorsal fin on their back. This keeps them stable and balanced. This is especially important when a shark is racing to catch its next meal!

Great white sharks also have gills on both sides of their body. Gills are holes that take in oxygen and release carbon dioxide. This is how they are able to breathe underwater.

Some animals such as penguins can walk and swim. Penguin feet are webbed like flippers. This helps them move quickly through the water and walk on land.

Penguins can shoot themselves out of the water, launching several feet into the air!

Handy Swimming

The handfish has a unique way of getting around. Even though it swims like other fish, it has also developed fins that allow it to walk along the ocean floor. This adaptation helps it hunt the small critters it eats.

handfish

High Flyers

There's one more place you can find animals—the sky! Animals that fly above us have adapted to life in the air in amazing ways.

Birds come in many different shapes, sizes, and colors. These are all physical adaptations that help them survive. Birds have wings that flap up and down. This lifts their bodies into the sky. Wings are important for a bird, but wings aren't the only adaptation needed for flight. Birds also have hollow bones. This makes them lighter. You've probably noticed that birds are usually covered in feathers. Feathers are light but still tough and strong. These adaptations require less energy for a bird to fly, which allows birds to travel longer distances.

If you look closely at a bird, you'll notice they have interesting tails. Their tails are like boat rudders. This helps birds change direction quickly. A bird's body is perfectly adapted for flight!

Finger Wings

The award for most unusual wings goes to bats! Bats have enlarged fingers that are attached by a web of skin. This gives them more control over their flexible wings, which allows them to make steep twists and turns.

Mid-Flight Nap

Albatross have wings that can extend up to 3.5 meters (11 feet)! These impressive birds may only return to the land every couple of years. For most of their lives they fly over the ocean. Albatross can even sleep while flying.

Hummingbirds can fly backwards.

Desert Survivalists

Deserts are hot, dry, and windy. Survival can be tough. Desert plants and animals have special adaptations to help them live in this harsh environment. Camels have thick eyebrows and long eyelashes that protect their eyes. They also have nostrils that can open and close to prevent sand from flying in!

Plants have also adapted to live in this extreme environment. All plants need water to survive. Desert plants have developed unique ways to get water. Most cactuses have long roots. But they don't grow deep underground. Instead, the roots remain close to the surface. This way, the roots can soak up the smallest bit of rain.

The gila monster stores fat in its thick tail to use as a backup food source.

What's in the Hump?

Did you know that the humps on a camel's back store fat, not water? They allow camels to survive up to two weeks without needing food or water!

Many plants that live in the desert have glossy leaves that reflect heat from the sun to keep cool.

Hunters

We know it's important for animals to eat. But animals can't drive to the grocery store and shop like humans can. Instead, animals have to find their own food to survive. Some animals, such as lions, are **carnivores**. Carnivores eat meat. To survive, carnivores must be strong hunters.

Tigers are skilled hunters. They're very intelligent and use their brains to outsmart their prey. They can even monitor things like wind direction to prevent prey from smelling them. They also have good hearing and can hear very soft sounds. This helps them narrow in on their prey. Then, they pounce.

The Venus flytrap is a meat-eating plant. Its leaves are lined with little hairs that trigger it to close when an insect touches them.

A Dangerous Invitation

Animals have developed surprising ways to trap their prey. Spiders weave large webs that are nearly invisible—until you're trapped inside!

Hasselt's spiny spider

Gray wolves are also predators. They hunt in packs, which is a behavioral adaptation. By working together, gray wolves can attack animals that are much larger than themselves. They often attack from the side or behind, catching their prey off guard!

Owls hunt at night. They have keen eyesight that allows them to see movement in the dark. Their eyes are twice as sensitive as ours! Like most carnivores, they have sharp claws. This helps them tear up their food.

Camouflaged Tricksters

Plants and animals have found clever ways to hide from predators. One way is by blending into the environment with camouflage. Creatures have different ways to camouflage themselves. Some can even change the color or texture of their skin.

Octopuses are masters of this technique. They are colorblind. But they're able to match the color, pattern, and texture of their skin to surrounding rocks. This ability helps them look like their environment so larger animals have a difficult time seeing them. This also helps them sneak up on their prey undetected.

Some rabbits, such as the snowshoe hare, have fur that can change color depending on the season. When it's summer, their fur is brown. But in the winter, their fur turns white so it blends in with the snowy landscape. Predators find it difficult to track them.

Now You See Me, Now You Don't

Jaguars live in the bottom layer of the rainforest. The coloring of the leaves in this area matches its fur and allows it to go unnoticed.

Camouflage can also distract a hunting predator. Some butterflies, such as the owl butterfly, have large spots on their wings, which resemble giant eyes. This confuses hunters into thinking they are a much larger creatures. In return, hunters keep their distance. These adaptations help animals blend into their natural habitat. But what happens when a habitat changes? Camouflage is specific to the habitat of the animal—it would be useless somewhere else!

coral shrimp

Chameleons don't change color to blend in to their environment—they change color with mood.

Fair-Weather Friends

When it's cold outside, you wear a warm coat. But animals can't throw on a winter parka. They must adapt to the **climate** of their environment to survive.

Depending on the location where the animal lives, the climate may be freezing cold or scorching hot. Adaptations vary depending on the animal and the habitat. Arctic foxes live in very cold climates. They have thick fur coats to protect them from icy conditions. They can survive in temperatures as low as -50° Celsius (-58° Fahrenheit)!

Arctic fox

Stay Cool, My Friend

An African bullfrog buries itself in the mud and makes a cocoon out of mucus to protect itself from the heat. This is called *estivation*. During estivation, it goes into a deep sleep. It can spend up to a year in this state!

African bullfrog

Sea creatures need to stay warm, too! Seals and whales have a layer of fat called *blubber* to help **insulate** their bodies. Blubber also helps these sea dwellers stay buoyant, or are able to float.

Not all animals have thick fur and a layer of blubber. But that doesn't mean they aren't able to stay warm. They must use their brains, or **instincts**, to keep them alive. For example, many types of birds migrate. They fly south during the winter to a warmer location. Then, when the summer months bring warmer weather, they return home.

Don't Freeze!

Many cold-blooded animals, such as lizards, have adapted to survive in freezing temperatures. To prevent the water in their blood from freezing, their bodies add more sugar and glycerol, a sugary alcohol, to their blood.

Reproduction

A species must reproduce to continue to exist. Reproduction is when an organism produces offspring. Animals choose their **mates** based on the most desirable traits. For prey, this could mean the animal with the best camouflage or one that can climb the highest. For predators, this could mean the animal with the sharpest teeth or that is the most aggressive. These desirable traits are then passed on to their offspring.

Once an animal has picked the best mate, they have to attract them. Some animals attract their mates in colorful ways. Male peacocks show off their brightly colored feathers to females. In return, females know the males are ready to mate. Female peacocks have more modest feathers that are camouflaged so they can blend in with surroundings while protecting their young.

Honk, Honk

Penguins attract their mates by making loud sounds. Male penguins stay in one place and call out. When females find them, they stand in front of one another and bow. A couple only sees each other once a year at mating time!

Flowering plants also reproduce to pass useful traits to the next generation. However, plants do not mate. Instead, they **pollinate**, usually with the help of insects. Many flowers have brightly colored petals to attract insects. Along with insects, wind and water help move pollen from one flower to the next. Once pollen moves from one flower to another flower of the same species, reproduction can begin.

Bird Designer

The male bowerbird attracts a mate by building and decorating a small hut. The bird then decorates it with flowers, leaves, and even caterpillar feces, which to a bird are quite alluring! To ensure that it gets the female and no one else does, it destroys other males' huts in its free time.

Animals have developed ways to protect their young. These adaptations are essential to the survival of a species. They ensure newborns survive. Humans protect and take care of their young until they are grown and can take care of themselves. However, some organisms give little attention to their newborns. Frogs and tortoises abandon their eggs right after laying them. They lay many eggs at one time, making it likely some of them will survive on their own. Many insects don't protect or care for their young either. Young insects rely on their habitat for everything they need to live.

Contrary to insects, mammals and birds rely on parents for survival. Most young mammals are unable to get food on their own. Mothers provide babies with nutrients through milk. This keeps babies healthy and full.

Baby elephants are born blind. These babies rely on their mother and herd to protect them. The herd watches over the babies. The mother will then eat a lot of food so she can produce milk for her baby. It's a team effort to raise a baby elephant!

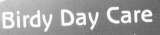

Birdy Day Care

Birds go to great lengths to protect their young. They find a secure location and build a sturdy nest to house their fledglings.

Mama's Boy

Orangutan babies cling to their mothers for the first four months of life—they never break contact! The mother nurses her baby until it is around five years of age. Since orangutans can only have babies every six to seven years, each mother and baby spend a lot of time together.

Embracing Change

Adaptations happen slowly over many generations. Camels have adapted to live in dry, hot environments. Their traits allow them to survive.

But what if an organism's environment changes? Things change all the time. Forests are chopped down. Weather shifts. When this happens, organisms can stay and adapt or they can leave and find new homes that will better suit their needs. If they can't do either of these things, they won't survive.

When organisms adapt to their new environments, they must find new ways to survive. They must find their niche. They may adapt with physical changes. They may adapt with behavioral changes. From a tiny ant in your backyard to the elusive jaguar in the jungles, all animals rely on adaptations. Organisms must always be prepared to adapt to change. Embracing this change will help them survive.

Javan Rhino

Poachers, or hunters, kill Javan rhinos for their horns. This is one factor that has forced the animal onto the endangered species list.

Time for a Change

For centuries, humans have changed the environments animals live in. We cut down forests and throw trash into animals' homes. Many animals cannot adapt quickly enough to survive the harsh conditions. Here are some ways you can help out:

- Visit a national park to learn more about the local species of plants and animals.

- Plant a tree.

- Join a wildlife-preservation group.

- Plant native plants.

- Reduce, reuse, and recycle.

tarsier

One-third of the amphibians in the United States are threatened by extinction.

27

Think Like a Scientist

How does blubber work? Experiment and find out!

What to Get

- 2 gallon-sized plastic bags
- big bowl or bucket
- duct tape
- ice cubes
- shortening
- spoon
- water

What to Do

1. Fill a bowl halfway with cold water. Add ice cubes.

2. Fill a large plastic bag with three to four scoops of shortening.

3. Place your hand inside the other plastic bag. Push your "gloved" hand into the bag filled with shortening. Smooth and squish the shortening around your hand until it is completely covered.

4. Gently pull your hand out of both bags. Take the inner bag and fold it over the top of the outer bag. Duct-tape the two together so that the shortening cannot escape.

5. Put your hand back into the inner bag. Carefully place your covered hand into the ice-cold water.

6. How does your hand feel? Now, place your other hand in the water. Which hand stays warmer longer?

Glossary

adapt—to change so that it is easier to live in a particular place

carnivores—living things that only eat meat

climate—the usual type of weather a place gets

habitat—the place where a plant or animal normally lives or grows

instincts—ways of behaving, thinking, or feeling that are not learned

insulate—to keep heat from being lost

mates—animals that produce young together

niche—an environment that has all the things that a particular plant or animal needs in order to live

offspring—the young of a plant or animal

pollinate—to give a plant pollen from another plant of the same kind so that seeds will be produced

predators—animals that live by killing and eating other animals

species—a group of plants or animals that are similar and can produce young

traits—qualities that make living things different from one another

Index

Handy Adaptations

Discover what it's like to have a bird's beak or cat's claws. Try picking up items such as cereal, lettuce, and water with tools such as an eyedropper, a spoon, tongs, and tweezers. Which tools made picking up the different items easier for you? Which tool works best for each item?